Ink and Chaos
Taila Cantrell

Tails Tales

Contents

For the girls with fire in their blood, tears in their eyes,

and rage in their hearts.

A Letter From Taila

Welcome Readers,

Words and stories have been my life for so long I forget the days before I had them, before I had immersed myself in fantasy worlds to escape. Even after I quit running from all the things that had broken me the stories had already woven themselves into my being, words and ink became my soul. For the first time collected into one place, I want to share with you the journey of my life through the poetry I wrote. It mostly ranges from age seventeen to somewhere in my early twenties. I can't tell you when all of these were written originally, but they will show you pieces of me that have never before seen the light of day. It's raw and vulnerable, and while I usually heavily edit my work, I've left these mostly as they were written. A homage to the girl I was once, and the woman I have now become. I won't pretend that what you'll find in these pages is beautiful, lyrical prose, but it is real. These are "poems", snippets of thoughts, emotions, and ideas that needed to be let out of the mind of a girl whose words were haunted.

If you see yourself within these pages, know that you are not alone. The pain you carry, the romance you crave, it is normal and natural. Never let anyone tell you differently. And most importantly? Never give up on your dreams. One day, you'll look back and see all that you have accomplished and know that it was meant to be.

-Taila Cantrell

Queen of Worlds

Queen of Nothing: At least that is what they tell me. Scream it until echoes across the stone. A tempo I am forced to believe.

Queen of Death: I've heard them whisper, their fear permeating the air. Why would they fear me if I am nothing?

Queen of Love: I've heard them claim myths were written about my love. 'It toppled empires' they whisper, but I can hear them. Love is a concept I have long since forgotten.

Queen of Fire: They yell as I exit my prison, my steps falling heavy. I feel the fire they speak of as I open my parched mouth.

Queen of Monsters: Of all the things they have claimed of me this surprises me the least. I feel like a monster as I take back my throne.

Queen of Mercy: I forgive them their sins as I take back my kingdom. It is not my place to punish them.

Queen of Stupidity: Words whispered by an enemy who shoves their dagger deeper into my back. I smile, knowing they have already lost.

Queen of Bone: My followers scream as I pass, cheering. I do not deserve their praise. My crown is made of bone, I do not wish to wear it. I have had no choice.

Queen of Worry: I watch as my children go to battle, wearing this title with pride. No one can claim I have no heart. I have fought our battles until the wicked end.

Queen of Life: Ironic they choose this name so close to the end. I have no time to embrace such things any longer.

Queen Eternal: I can hear their cries at my death. 'Do not leave us'. My parting words are of love. 'I will return'.

Lost Queen

I wonder what they will say, when they learn what they
have truly lost?

Their Queen will soon be dead, do they wonder where
she is?

Lost in seas they will never find.

She can no longer protect them.

I wonder when they will realize she planned to die?

That she did not want to stay with them.

She hated her life.

I wonder when she will figure out what she left behind?

That she already had what she searched for.

Will they mourn or rejoice?

I wonder what her final thoughts were?

Regret or Peace?

My Valkyrie

How can anyone claim that I am not a warrior? That the very scent of blood does not cling to my skin. That battles have not been etched into my bones.

How can anyone claim that you are not Death? Who else could glide into a bloodbath, looking so angelic. Calm, but innocent. I remember the blood dripping from my fingers as you made your way toward me.

I have heard the stories of the Valkyries who whisked warriors to Valhalla, but I never expected to be taken. I am not a woman who forgives, nor do I regret the things I have done. And yet you still flew me away.

I could not unnerve you with my sharp teeth and love of dark things, not with my scarred chest and cold eyes.

Not even my silver tongue took you by surprise. I do not know what to make of you.

I cannot leave the battle. War is all I've ever known. How could you expect me to stay here with you? Darling, I cannot be killed. My soul longs for the bloodshed you have taken me from.

Valhalla is not the place for me, love. You are a golden sun, and I am nocturnal. I should not yearn for your light, it is not meant for a woman like me.

I have been bathed in blood, I cannot ask the gods to give you to me. War is the song of my heart, the very air that I breathe. Please do not expect me to leave my roots behind.

How can anyone claim that you did not change me? I have always fought my battles with zeal, but after you I fight differently. I no longer wish to feel the sword against my own skin. Once again I am on the battlefield, blood dripping, as you glide toward me. But now? You are here with me.

You have become the reason I fight.

Icarus

My dear Icarus,

How could you fly me into the sun with you? How could you allow me to burn in your place? My tongue tastes of ashes, I know it is the taste of you.

My Icarus... how much of a lie those words turned out to be. You could never belong to anyone. Oh how I wished I had listened to the gods sooner.

I bare your scars now, Icarus, but I can never truly take your place. Your wings must burn. You melt off of me. Oh sweet, Icarus, so young. Cheeks filled with the glow of youth. I've been tricked.

Untitled

The old gods would be disappointed, but we are the young gods and we have forgotten. No one cares for the old ways anymore. We are too busy concerning ourselves with mortal pains and pleasures to save ourselves. We will die horrid deaths, just as our predecessors, and we will cry out. Do we deserve our fates when we were not taught any differently. The old gods are dead. They were once as we are now, stupid and reckless. They did not learn from their mistakes. Why haven't we? We will suffer if history repeats itself. Will our children rise up and kill us as we once did? Can we truly blame them if they do? We do not have an eternity, but we often behave as if we do.

We will never learn.

Persephone/Beast

Persephone

They claim she was unwilling. Naive and Childlike. But they forgot her very name means annihilate. She wondered down into Hell, and found love.

The myths are wrong. She was Queen of Death and Goddess of Spring. Feared and Revered.

They forgot who her father was. King of the Gods. She favored him. Destined to rule.

Her husband meek in comparison. Her iron fist was loved by all. Far more formidable than any other god. With flowers in her hair.

A soul made of light, dearly loved by the dark. She was her happiest wrapped in shadow.

Beast

They believe my husband to be the monster. They believe my meek appearance is who I am. They have not noticed my sharp teeth and claws.

They should appeal to him. For he is the merciful one. They fear him, they should fear me. I will remove the skin from their bones for my beast.

I wear the horns in this relationship. My beast wants to live in peace, and I will kill to make sure that happens.

Tragic Heroes

You move like a predator, but I can see the truth. Your claws are fake. Your teeth filed to a point. You are playing a game you do not know the rules to, and I have no interest in teaching you.

I'm sure someday you will learn. Like all the great heroes you will find that you are not the biggest and baddest in our world. No one truly fears you. No one truly loves you.

You are Achilles. Invincible, yet dead.

You are Hercules. Your family is dead, and you've gone insane.

History will not even remember you, because you are not special. Heroes are a dime a dozen in our world.

They won't remember your name. The people you saved died painful deaths, screaming.

Iron

I think they forgot that our very blood is metal. Iron straight into our hearts. They may think they'll win, but we know they will have to bleed us to do so.

We aren't afraid to die.

We will bleed to save our families from the horror. We are forged from a fire they will never understand. Steel beaten until it can hold up against anything.

Guilt

There were days I did not think we would make it.

Days filled with the screams of the damned. Now those

screams only haunt our dreams. Blood dripping in guilt

conscious's. It does not matter who we did to survive.

We're still alive, and they aren't.

At least that's what we tell ourselves in the dark.

No one asks, and we don't tell. Would it be easier to just

forget? We pretend we don't hear each other screaming

at night. Sometimes I wish I was back there, at least the

evil made sense. We had each other then, now we're truly

alone.

This seems too much like limbo. Neither living nor dead.

We avoid each other, pray that we don't have to notice

how deep the bags under our eyes are. I know they notice.

Sometimes I still can feel the cold steel, and my own warm blood. I pretend I don't.

It was easier when we could pretend we were innocent. That we did nothing wrong in escaping. But who did we leave behind?

Survival

They do not know how much we listen to our primal
instincts. They cannot figure out why the run from us,
why they cannot meet our eyes. They don't know how
much we love it when they flee. Like prey.

I've heard them claim we are not animals, but I think
they forget how basic our instinct to survive is. We are
predators. Begging to sink our teeth into things. To fight
and fuck. To eat and sleep. We wish for nothing more.

They try to make us forget who we are.

We are the top of the food chain, and they have forgotten
how to roar.

Untitled

There are so many things left to say. To much time
wasted. So many things forgotten, left behind. Never to
be examined again.

Is it fair? Well, life isn't fair. It takes everything from us.
Love, Time, Trust. At least it never deprives us death. And
yet, it gives us all of those things first.

Forgetting is the tragedy of being human. I pray everyday
that I do not forget anything. That I remember every
heartbreak, horror, laugh, tear, celebration. I don't want
to forget the way your hair shines in the sunlight, the way
she smiles as if she doesn't have a care in the world. The
way my heart faces in anticipation.

I want to remember everything, so no one can ever tell me I haven't loved, lost, and loved again.

Trapped

I am trapped in a garden, surrounded by beautiful flowers,
but trapped none the less. Stuck between thorns and
stinging branches. No one leaves this garden, but then
again all enter willingly. Or at least that's what we're told.
I don't believe them, why would I come here willingly.
I have known freedom, I would not want to be trapped
once again. No, my will had nothing to do with this.
Laughter echoes. I should not remember, but I will not
escape.

Did I sacrifice myself for someone else?

Who did I love enough to lose my freedom for? I have
forgotten their face. Did they love me?

Do they know I am in this garden.

Trapped. Trapped. Trapped.

Remember

Remember

Please do not forget, because one day I will have no choice. You have to remember for their sake, someday they will need you.

They mustn't lose us both.

Please forgive my absence. Do not let your heart begin to hate me. Do not lose yourself because I am gone. I will miss you with every shred of my being. Even if I have forgotten your face I will remember your soul.

I'm begging you.

I hate to beg.

Remember

Master

They have forgotten who their master is. I am at fault,
I did not leave any of myself behind for them. They
suffer because of me. They should not be punished for
my inaction.

I am here now. It is time for them to put away their
childish qualms. I have come for them. I will fight to
regain their trust. Their place is at my side.

You will not take them from me. They are not yours to
have. They are my angels, created for me.

'Come home.' I beg them. The time nears. I do not wish
to replace you, but I will if I must.

Stranger

Recently I remembered what it was like to be me. I woke up, and suddenly I was back in my body, sitting up in bed, all the ghosts had left.

I know I left for a while, let another part of myself take over so I could cope with it all. I worked to remember, I went back to the very roots of my person, and found who I was.

I've aged since the last time I was here. Not much, but I can feel that my soul has been through more, seen more, done more. It's harder settling back into myself, but it was worth it.

Worth it to remember who I am, who I was, who I will be. Getting back to basics was everything I needed.

Names

Brie

I knew her. I can still see her golden skin bathed in

sunlight, God kissing her with light. Red hair, her fire

bird soul come to life.

Laughter echoing through the crowded halls we so often

walked together.

They stole something from her. Her light faded. The

phoenix cannot rise from these ashes.

Alexander

You, so much like the king you were named after. Proud, brave, golden haired, and the end of a dynasty. You wanted everyone at your feet, and I refuse to kneel for anyone.

I was always a different person when we were together. Something about you brought out the beastly parts of me. I never recognized myself after our time together, and it was addictive to become someone else.

We were toxic, and it was everything I needed.

Mr. Smith

Funny that I can only think of you by your title.

No warmth, no familiarity so unlike our relationship.

Now I hold no joy for those moments. No interest in you.

I don't even know why I'm writing this.

Melonie

We were such opposites.

I was fire and you were ice.

Your apathy did not match my passion.

I will never understand how we worked, I guess we didn't. Your ice froze me out, and my fire burned you away.

Violence Saga

Jubilee

You scare me. Not in the ways you should, no the vio-
lence calls to me. You scare me, because I can see how
you could so easily wreck my heart.

It wouldn't be difficult even, for you to step around the
walls I've spent years building.

I always said I would need someone who could stabilize
me, but then I found you. Or did you find me? I don't
remember, but it doesn't matter now anyway.

You will never be my sun, no my planet will spin out of
control in your orbit. But I wonder if that's exactly what
I need.

Lose a little control, float among the stars without a care.

But inevitably I will crash back down, covered in black
star dust, trying desperately to remember who I am. It is

not in my nature to let go, to be out of control, but with

you I can almost imagine it working.

Maybe our souls will circle for a little while, enjoying the

way they mesh together. Broken.

Violence I

I should avoid your violence, I'm too easily sucked into

the way it feels to release that anger. To be around some-

one who isn't afraid of the blood lust. Because, god, I want

to fuck you while blood is dripping off my teeth. Because

I'd never be afraid of hurting you. Because I'd reveal in

the chaos we could create.

Let's be beastly together.

I wonder if the sound of you breaking someone would

turn me on? If the chaos of my being would find its silence

in your violence?

Maybe we'll find out. Watch as you fight, maybe I'll feed my own lust, let my nails rip into someone's skin. Chaos and violence feeding me.

The sound of flesh hitting flesh like music to my ears. Wonder if you realize? I'd probably let you fuck me into oblivion after, knuckles bruised, someone's else blood drying on your skin. Bruise me if you want, I don't care. But don't forget that later, I will remind you. Remind you that I am not breakable, that I am just capable of leaving marks as you. That there is a reason you chose me. Maybe we'll stay sated for a while, but the violence, the chaos, it can only stay away so long. Inevitably we'll return to it.

Violence II

We both know violence is not poetic, as much I write about with flourish, with pretty words, it isn't beautiful.

Not when you're sitting in the shower, water so hot

it burns, while you scrub your skin until the normal

pinkness turns almost as red as the blood dripping in your

conscious.

It's the way my hands are shaking as I write this. It's

spending days watching them shake uncontrollably be-

cause the need to release the extra energy is so strong.

It's avoiding alcohol, because I don't trust myself. It's

hiding when the mood to walk my bloody boots into

your apartment and fuck you strikes.

It is having so few fears you scare the people you love.

Because if you can survive everything you already have,

when death was so close, why be afraid at all? It's people

pointing out your 'vibe' or 'murder walk', it's the 'you

smile like you bite' or the 'you scared me when I first you.'

It will always be the first thing people notice about you;

your violence.

I know it can't possibly last, violence and chaos are un-

sustainable. Like a hurricane that will wreak havoc, but

ultimately fizzle out. Because no one can maintain my
level of chaos forever.

It's easy to get lost in, my brand of release and relief.

People don't realize they've done it until it's too late.

You are a paradox to me. The violence, the anger, all of
that I can understand, I can relate, but the other half, the
neediness, the sweetness. I find myself afraid to admit that
I have no idea how to handle it.

No one has ever sought comfort from me, they do not
know the parts of me that are loving, because there's too
much risk and vulnerability in love.

Blood Lust

I've always struggled to contain my anger. Avoiding
confrontation when possible, knowing that the way it
boils out of me isn't healthy.

The way tears rush down my face in anger, throws you
off the first time it happens. Maybe because you're so used
to my coldness, to my need for blood. You didn't realize
that I could even cry.

I avoid you occasionally, because I feel myself becoming
less guarded, more honest. Can't let you see my dis-
comfort. In trying to keep the facade alive I destroy it,
showing the heart tucked in my black deck of cards.
But I always resort back to the blood lust, because I trust
it to protect me. I can stalk the streets alone, watch people
move away from me, knowing I'm seeking something...
dangerous. Let the pounding music in my ears wash way
the fears your interest causes me.
It should have been simple to push you away. The way I
shake constantly, the heat, my bite, my voice, my faked

apathy. All of it should have been the perfect recipe to drive you away.

But you don't seem to care that sometimes I have a fire in my eyes that lends so closely to madness. You ignore my awkward attempts to brush you off, the bitchiness. It doesn't seem to faze you.

Why do you have to remind me of him? I can't exactly pinpoint a specific trait that you share, but I feel it in my bones when I talk to you. I wonder if it's some kind of divine punishment. To torture my blood lust with the flairs of protectiveness. I want to stop people from hurting you, and that worries me.

Because I also want you to protect me, and I've never needed protection before. I have too much blood lust to be protected.

Chaos

You ignore my chaos, maybe you are too wrapped up in your own to recognize my instability. Or maybe that's the very reason you stick around. See how far my violence goes. See if I can equal you, fulfill some need for attention you have.

I am my father's daughter, too loud, too angry, prepared to do anything to survive. I can't be like her. I am not sweet, I do not need you, I value my independence too much to let you have all of me. I am not pliable, I cannot be shaped into the perfect girlfriend.

I will fight you, and I'll win because I can't let you be in control. It's too dangerous, handing over every piece of me to anyone.

No ring will ever sit upon my finger, proudly declaring that I am owned. I am not a prize to be won, no one would want the type of damage I come with anyway. And yet, you haven't run away. I have no idea how to cope with that.

You've made promises you can't possibly keep, but a part of me almost wants to believe you. But I can't be fooled, no one stays, so neither will you.

I can't let myself fall, because my chaos enjoys you. I can feel that part of me begging for you. It's distracting, because it demands too much. It wants to own, to remind that I am always in control.

It's my shaking hands, desperately fidgeting because I want so badly to slap you. To wrap a hand around your throat, while straddling your lap. Bite you until your breath is coming in fast pants. Swallow your cries, laugh at the way you squirm.

Don't worry I'll make sure you enjoy it.

Remember pain and pleasure are a very fine line.

Fang

I earned every fang in my bloody mouth. I earned every scar and raw throat. I earned my viciousness. I cannot be soft, the person capable of that was lost long ago.

The Tide

You can't breathe; the strong hand wrapped around your throat pressed ever so carefully. You stare into ocean eyes, deep and dark, captivating like the sky. You take pleasure in driving him to a breaking point, forcing him to lose control, such well-maintained control. Who are you to break him, to be broken by him?

Things reach a fever pitch, pounding hearts, teeth gripping a pillow, trying desperately to hide the sounds. Dare to be loud, let them hear those animalistic sounds, rip the clothes from your bodies, violent and beautiful. Nails bite into skin, some part of you longs to run, to fight the feeling just a little longer. He drags it out of you, screaming and soaked. Tides clashing.

The moon controls the tide, always pushing and pulling it away. He is only worshipping at the feet of the most powerful force in this universe. Trapped between your hips, cradling life itself.

Casket

My casket calls me, a siren song, ever entrancing. Years and years of willpower against it, tied to the beams of a ship I never chose to be on. There are days where I feel it hover, Death watching, waiting to welcome me home. It would take so little, and yet, hesitation has always stopped me. As if Life, flowers in her hair, is fighting for me, begging me to see it through until the end. It's a lovers embrace, a mothers embrace, a promise that the call is nothing more than lies.

I am tired. The casket is my eternal bed, giving me relief for the first time. No dreams.

Forget

The world is designed to make you forget your divinity.
Forces us to suppress our rage, our lust, anything that
could fuel us. Force us to work our bodies and minds into
exhaustion. Keep us fighting over pointless things so we
never unlock our true potential.

I'm a Goddess, built in perfection, wrapped in unholiness.
I will not be stripped of my power, it is intrinsic. No God
nor man could take it. It is built into the very foundation
of my soul.

Untitled

When you feel like you're needed. You don't have to worry about being wanted.

Divinity

The pain in our lack of divinity is haunting. We are

not old gods, reincarnated to new purpose. We are not

fae, dancing in the forest, luring in the mortals. We are

not dragons, hoarding our riches, breathing fire on our

enemies. No magic still exists in this world, it is stifling,

the humid air crushing our lungs.

We are the monsters, the villains of the story, crushing

and bashing everything that gives us life, that breaths

hope into this universe. We cannot allow life to exist

without pain. We're not even special in our evils.

The dreamers, those of us born with stars in our eyes,

that breathe in magic at our first breath. We become de-

stroyed, tortured, ripped up filth on the street. Doormats

to the worst of the universe. We're not allowed to create

change, to heal the curses set around us.

Burnt

What's the point of burning down a kingdom already ruins? Why turn crumbling buildings to ash. There was no shining eyes, and children's laugh here. Why March an army down already empty and decimated streets.

Curse

The Cursed

You won't know peace, but you may impart it on others.

Visions will haunt you, the energy will catch you off guard.

Your words will scare people, horrify them when they come to fruition.

Loneliness will permeate every corner of your life, the few that stay you will push away.

The true curse, you feel, so strongly it tortures you. You feel with a vibrancy few can imagine.

The Seer

It's inherited, the way that you see, a generational curse, though it's often framed like a blessing.

It will not be your only gift, just the strongest. The older you are, the more it shows itself.

In the hardest of times, the visions, the knowing will be

almost without pause.

The path will seem foggy and dark at times, you will

bring light to others, answers to some.

They won't always believe you. Another cross to bear.

The Gift

You can see the corners of people, their dark motivations.

You can protect those who listen.

The knowing is a boon, used wisely, your dreams will

come to fruition.

You will recognize those who are meant for you with

ease. Love a recompense for your suffering.

You are comfortable with the darkness of your gift, it

nourishes you.

Slowly, almost imperceptibly, you will fall in love with

your sight. Rely on it more than the oxygen in your lungs

Untitled

I don't think it's the usual creeping edginess. This feels

like change, unwavering. Like a black, crashing tide.

Planning to drown us all, drag us into the abyss.

I can't say I'm scared, I'm used to the drowning. To the

flailing worry, the claws forever dug deep into my chest.

I think the life raft would the the true horror, the illusion

of safety, even as the monsters lurk just under your feet.

I dont live in delusion, unaware, maybe that isn't for the

best. Maybe the deluded have been gifted peace beyond

what the rest of us can understand.

I've watched others be rescued on boats, lights and heli-

copters, flashing to save them as they inhale the blackness

down into their lungs. Gasping. Reaching. Always reach-

ing.

I don't know panic like that, the water has always been home to me. The safety is unknown. Better the monsters we know, than the evil unseen.

Maybe I am meant for the depths, the constant battle, it feels natural.

Them

He is cracked bones and crooked teeth, not pretty or alluring. She is smoke and moonlight, ephemeral at the very best. One so hard to catch, to collar and own, too busy dancing in rain to care either way. The other calm and quiet. He is seeking, searching, never quite finding answers to questions he doesn't know to ask. And the collision is closer to train wreck than heavens glory. Teeth gnash, tears spill, throats burning from words screamed. The earth didn't move when they met, but the stars gave a quiet sigh, as though things were finally just right. She was no Goldilocks, and he wasn't the Bear, but somehow they fit together, their sins bared.

Feeling

I chase feeling like it's the last drop of water in the desert.

Freight Train

I don't know how to avoid being a wrecking ball, freight train girl. I don't know how to be soft or easy or submissive. I've always been chaos and destruction. Those things are as natural as breathing. I can turn life upside down, can make storm clouds on sunny days. Smoke, ashes, tears, pain, it's everything I've always known. Even the things I create begin with destruction. Because everything has to change, to be molded through suffering, through degradation and pain, to be worth anything. If not then I've been through Hell, and gained no knowledge from it.

Because if I am not allowed creation, I will destroy everything. And isn't that the very same thing.

Cold

Becoming cold was unexpected. I've been hot my entire life. Hot blooded. Hot headed. Always burning. I don't know when the ice started to encroach. Cannot pinpoint the moment I became frozen. I still rage inside. The inferno still licks underneath my skin, but it is met with chilling control.

Predator vs Prey

Predators don't tell their prey they are predators.

Prey knows to be afraid. To hide. To listen. To be hyper

vigilant.

There is an order to these things.

A cycle that has lasted for thousands of years, millennia

even.

Soldier

Soldier.

I heard the words, 'you've always been my solider." It hit me in the chest, absorbed in the swirling pit that lives in my soul, becoming a part of me in a way statements like this do. My minds eye cried, my inner child cringed at the thought. My inner teenager teeth bared took the words like a badge of honor. Always ready to rip someone apart, to feel blood and bones under my fists. My soul feel tired, yet unwavering as always. We all know what this means. There is pride here. There is hurt here. But we press on, move on from it at the time. Because we have to keep fighting.

Fighter.

As peace looms ever near, there is a restlessness. A discomfort. Something new always comes. Be it battle with my own mind, or something else. I don't have an off switch, there is always something to fight. Those may be smaller now, the intricate game of adulthood, more challenging than expected. It doesn't come as naturally, we were built to fight. To win battles, not sit quietly down, to raise a family, to pursue dreams. I guess that was what winning was for, but it doesn't feel real.

Strategist.

The leftover ways of warriors. Always carefully crafting moves to advance, willing to do anything to obtain our goals. This is not stress, it's peace for us. Other people don't comprehend it. Tell us this isn't how life is supposed to be, that we are "unhealthy". What beauty it is to be built another way. To know peace, love, calmness. We envy it. But we have no shame in who we are. If you are always prepared to fight, then you are never caught off guard. Hypervigilance is the way. It isn't a switch we turn on and off when we need it.

Forgiveness

We have to forgive ourselves. The path of healing, of accepting and improving ourselves, to admitting everything we've done wrong. That has been done wrong to us. It isn't always about forgiving others. Sometimes it is. Sometimes you have to let the bitterness, hate, and anger fly away. To forgive the people that broke us, without that breaking we wouldn't be the people we are today, on the path set ahead of us. But healing the part of us that we damaged, the moments we chose to hurt ourselves, rather than hold our inner child's hand and be the person we needed, it will feel like light burning through us. It's okay to hurt, to cry and scream, and rip ourselves to shreds, but at some point the tears have to dry up, your throat is sore and your life is in tatters. And you have to choose.

How do you fix yourself, when suffering validates every horrible things everyone has said to you, and every evil thought inside your head?

Fire

The fire licks for hand, ever burning, palms unharmed, but the world around you turns to ash. I froze you, let my ice cool your heart, let your heat warm me for the first time in an eternity.

Left

To everyone who left,

The list keeps growing. Twenty years of people leaving should have taught me better lessons. But I'm so tired of having a guarded heart, of constantly waiting for the knife to nick my spine. I just want to trust people, to have a family, but I should know better. Should know that everyone leaves. Without exception. People love to argue that they will be the ones to stay. I should stop being gullible enough to believe them.

Many of you will blame me, I guess that easier, blaming other people for abandonment. Maybe you will instead rationalize, claim I never needed you, took you for granted too often, I am too emotional, too broken. You may not be wrong, the patterns revolves too closely around me. Maybe I unknowingly sabotage relationships. Let the negativity, the doubts plague my mind, until my behavior changes. Maybe I turn cold, or too hot. I'm not sure. Maybe I am a beacon to those who want to leave footprints across hearts, etching their names in marble, leaving marks.

Emotional

I've never been good at the emotional. I am not sweet or sappy by nature. I show affection through touch, through concern, sometimes in my weaker moments through hurt or anger, but I do not write love poems to people. Not to say I never speak of love with fanciful words, describing shining hair, freckles, the slight dimples in a lovers back, the physicality of love is the easiest to describe. But I do not speak words, do not validate feelings well, cannot express the height of my emotion. It is a weakness, a flaw in my ability to love. Maybe I can't write sappy love letters, because the little girl who had these abilities was crushed one too many times. Maybe my free-spirited nature is too afraid of being trapped by my own words. Feelings can be fleeting things. What if they change? I've never been willing to sacrifice my heart. Gotta protect the center. Protect the center, protect the soul. I know myself all too well. I will always chose people I love over myself.

Every time. No matter the consequences.

It isn't that I don't want to write you pretty words, flowing across the page in a sensual dance, reminding you of skin on skin, of stolen kisses and gasping sighs. I have always been a crafter of words, they've slipped off my tongue with ease, curling their way around necks. Fluttering wing words. Reminding you of me, even when you can no longer hear my voice, the words will haunt you. But I find myself tongue tied all too often, caught up in chaos, the words tripping, jumbling, mixing together until… there's a silence I very rarely reach. I know I have found it with you before. And maybe that silence can be enough.

Three

Three words...

Three words to remind you that you have no control.

Life will happen. Not every question can be answer.

Just three little words.

It Just Is.

Acknowledgements

I think I have to give an ode to the past in many ways here. Without it I would not be where I am today. Loss, grief, and pain are painted across the pages of this work (along with a touch of teen angst), but they have never defined who I am or who I can be. I have my grandmother to thank for that most of all. No matter what I went through, she was determined that it would not define my life. Without her unerring support I don't think I'd be alive today. I miss you everyday, Grammy.

To my husband, Tyler, who is a huge part of why I no longer write this type of poetry. Without him, I don't know that I would have ever published a single book. Now here I am, sharing my most intimate words with all of you. Thank you so much. Even in our worst moments, love has always triumphed.

And a thanks to the people who left me in my darkest moments, but most of all to the people who stayed. My family, Dad, Whitneigh, Papaw, and Teagan. Without them, I wouldn't be here, and I certainly wouldn't have the confidence to pursue my dreams.

And finally, to my street and ARC team, to Leah and Larisssa (my PA's), and as always to you, lovely reader, I hope you've come to the end of this small book a little more seen than you were before. Thank you for your continued support of my writing career.

About the author

In every story, Taila blends spellbinding romance with trauma, chaos, and hope. Her books remind readers that even in the darkest moments, the heart still remembers how to burn bright.

Taila Cantrell can be found lurking in the mountains of East Tennessee with her husband. Whether she's at her day job, wrangling the feral blue-collar men, tucked into a local bookstore, or at home curled up with her many cats and two pups, she's always plotting the next story. Her readers can look forward to many genres from fantasy romance to poetry to murder mysteries there is no story Taila isn't willing to give her voice to.

Also by

The Reclaiming Wonderland Series

Code Red

Code White: Frosted Wonderland

Blue Dreams

Emerald Knights (Coming April 2026)

The Austral Witches:

Primal Echoes

One Bloody Night

Two Shadowed Hearts

Three Little Doves (Coming February 2026)

Four Twisted Dreams (Coming March 2026)

The Tides of Desire Trilogy w/Allena Scott

A Tide of Secrets and Storms

www.ingramcontent.com/pod-product-compliance
Lightning Source LLC
Chambersburg PA
CBHW070646130626
46555CB00006B/2727